Financial Intelligence

The Ultimate Beginner Guide

Prem Amrit

ISBN 978-93-5667-056-3
© Prem Amrit 2022
Published in India 2022 by Pencil

A brand of

One Point Six Technologies Pvt. Ltd.
123, Building J2, Shram Seva Premises,
Wadala Truck Terminal, Wadala (E)
Mumbai 400037, Maharashtra, INDIA
E connect@thepencilapp.com
W www.thepencilapp.com

Author biography

Prem Amrit is an Investor, Digital Marketer, Social Media Marketer, graphic designer, website developer, and writer. He has started investing in the Indian stock market in 2020, and he has a successful history of finding some multibagger stocks.

CONTENTS

Foreword

It is important to set your financial priorities in life, as this can help secure your financial future. Improper handling of funds can be too stressful.

Many people do not know where and how they spend most of their income. How many times have you withdrawn money from an ATM, only to find out a few days later that there is none? It is often difficult to remember how much you have spent, and that money is often spent on frivolous purchases.

A budget will help avoid this by holding people accountable for the income they spend. If a person only has $50 a month left for food, they can opt out of buying a $3 designer coffee.

Chapter 1

Know your priorities and your Position

Double-check your finances! At the same time, be clear about your priorities. Some people make mistakes when it comes to prioritizing their finances, such as saving more for their kids' college education and less for their own retirement.

What are your main financial problems?
List your positive financial position in terms of income, debt management, and savings.
How do you think you got here – what changes do you want to see?
What are your organizational options in financial emergencies?
Write it down now: The amount we have invested in the emergency fund is _________.
How does your family deal with money problems: emotionally or rationally?
Who makes financial decisions? How did it get here? How many collaborations?

Why it matters:
Clarity and commitment. Authorities agree that families need to double-check their finances before jumping into

the numbers - the best chance of success occurs when both couples are involved.

Here, we will explain to you the basics of personal financial ratios and their analysis. This will help you keep a close eye on your personal finances.

Now you ask what is a personal financial ratio.

As the name suggests, these ratios refer to your personal wealth, assets, or cash. More importantly, they are very easy to understand. The simple discipline of budgeting both assets (what you earn or own) and liabilities (what you spend or owe others) will help you control your finances.

Here is a simple guide to help you understand these ratios in detail. Let's see how these ratios can help.

Basic solvency ratio

This ratio measures your ability to pay your monthly expenses in the event of any emergency or natural disaster. It is calculated by dividing the last money you have by your monthly expenses.

Basic solvency ratio = Cash / Monthly expenses

(this ratio is not expressed as a percentage). You can also call it emergency preparedness or emergency preparedness ratio. This ratio can help you prepare for the unexpected.

An illustration of a 30-year-old businessman whose wife had emergency gallbladder surgery last year. Although they had adequate insurance for such an eventuality, due to some administrative issues, he was told on the day of discharge that he had to pay in cash as the bill could not be paid.

He had difficulty placing funds in an emergency fund. He is lucky that he has good friends and relatives who lend him money. But not everyone has such big fans or relatives to save them in such a short time. I'm sure no one wants to wear the same pair of shoes.

So we have to arrange for this situation. As? By supporting an emergency fund!

Let's see how much money is enough. This is where the basic solvency ratio comes in handy.

The cash in the numerator (almost cash) of the basic solvency ratio formula typically includes the following:

savings account
Bank term deposit
Liquidity
cash on hand

The above items are current assets, and they will come in handy in case of financial problems. Liquidity can be delivered immediately. The same applies to term deposits, as they can be broken and liquidated immediately in an emergency.

Monthly cost:

For convenience, only mandatory fixed and variable commissions are used here. Entertainment fees are not charged, as these fees can be waived.

Mandatory fixed costs include income, credit, insurance, and the rent you pay.

On the other hand, mandatory variable fees include food, transportation, clothing/personal care, medical services, utilities, education, and various mandatory fees (the above may vary by individual).

Dividing the above amount by 12 (i.e. 12 months) will give you a monthly average as your variable costs may change. Assuming you have 60,000 in cash and your average monthly payment is 25,000, your basic solvency ratio would be calculated as: 60,000 / 25,000 = 2.4.

But is it really that great?

Incomplete. The ideal ratio should be 3.

What does the number 3 mean?

This means that you must have mandatory spending equal to or at least 3 months as an emergency fund or an emergency fund.

Why only 3 months? This is because studies show that 3 months is enough time to get out of any financial difficulty. As people approach retirement age, they should make sure to save this fund for up to six months for necessary expenses. Funds must be held fractionally in the form of cash, term deposits or working capital.

You must learn to prioritize your financial goals in order to stay happy and financially stable in old age. This does not mean that you do not think about the future of your child, but simply set your financial priorities.

Set a monthly amount for food, water and shelter as these are your basic needs. You need to consider buying a variety of healthy foods and try to avoid unnecessary unhealthy snacks. You should also do your best at your current job, as this is your source of income for utilities, mortgages or rent, and groceries. This is where you begin to clarify your priorities.

Some people are so frugal when it comes to grocery shopping that they ignore their health needs and just buy expensive gadgets or airline tickets for their leisure time. Keep in mind that it is your duty and priority to meet your daily needs so that you do not avoid rent or mortgages, utility bills and other things that are critical to well-being, especially if you have a family.

Sometimes this can be a cause of disagreement between

couples because they have different views on income management. Another wants to spend most of the money and is not afraid of financial debt, while another prefers to save some money for a rainy day or emergency. Be a good role model for your children, as they speak highly of you as a parent.

If you have credit card debt, pay off your credit card debt. Paying off the credit card with the highest interest rate and then the credit card with the lower interest rate is the best thing you can do to pay off all your credit card debt. Whenever possible, use cash to buy things or goods and control your spending habits.

Prevent overuse of your credit card, so you can continue to access your account when you really need it. Some of those who work never bothered to save for emergencies, abused their credit and now have nothing. You don't want to end up in a place where you have no income, or even lose access to your credit card because your account is closed.

Focus on saving up enough money for your emergency fund, especially once you've paid off all your credit card debt. This is very important in the event of a job loss or other major unforeseen event that could happen to you or anyone in your family. Avoid the temptation to buy things you can't afford and focus on building up savings for the unexpected.

Setting your financial priorities should be your main goal. Clearly list the key items that cover your monthly expenses and finances, and number each item from largest to smallest according to its importance and need.

If you already have enough cash savings for your emergency fund, increase your 401(k) or 403(b) contributions and retirement savings. Try to save 15-20% of your salary for retirement.

Save for retirement before saving for college. When your kids grow up, they can use student loans, get scholarships, or attend a more affordable, high-quality community college or state university. When you think about their future, you also need to think about your golden years.

Take advantage of free training. Participation in free seminars and trainings to improve your knowledge is a very good investment in your future. Since the job market is highly competitive, it is important to set career goals in life.

Amend or update your will, so your wishes are guaranteed and fulfilled. No matter how small your property is, you will need a property layout. Some people assume that their assets and property will automatically go to their families, but in the absence of a legal will, the state may intervene and distribute your property or inheritance.

Assess your insurance coverage. Make sure your auto and homeowner policies are up-to-date, and their deductibles are fair. If you are the head of the household and work full time, you can apply for life insurance. You may also consider purchasing long-term care insurance to help pay for care or living expenses in your old age.

Chapter 2

Keep Track and Set Limits

You may have thought you knew how much you spent on a super latte until you saw the numbers in front of you. For most people, that's a savings of $65 to $85 a month, or more than $750 a year. Leave Starbucks and eat out every day.

Look at non-monthly bills such as auto insurance, vehicle registration... Decide between need and desire.

Important information

In today's industry, few people take the time to develop a personal budget. Some people don't see the point in it, others just don't want to limit their spending habits.

With that in mind, it's no surprise that individual bankruptcies are at an all-time high. People have reached a point in our society where they buy on impulse without thinking about the outcome.

To reverse this trend, people need to be more responsible for their consumption patterns. One of the best tools to help a person achieve this behavior is a personal budget.

A personal budget is a financial plan that sets out the total amount of money that will be spent on each expense category in a given month. A useful budget will take into account factors such as the amount of income earned, retirement debt, retirement savings, and an emergency fund.

Budget benefits describe an accurate representation of how much consumer goods a person can afford. Whether it's a house, a car, or a new TV, people will be able to determine if a particular purchase fits within their monetary limits. This can be used as a precautionary measure to prevent financial problems.

It is important to understand that simply creating a budget is not enough. If he does not accustom himself to perseverance, this in itself will bring absolutely no personal benefit.

This can sometimes be very difficult, especially if a person has developed the habit of spending freely without thinking. However, the long-term benefits of financial freedom, debt-free living, and a comfortable retirement far outweigh any potential hardship.

List as many of these accounts as you can within 12 months.

Now, with the "twelfth" rule, money is set aside for these expenses each month to limit their impact when payments are due.

Then focus on where you can spend less without depriving yourself.

• What wasteful or indulgent habits can you cut? (Take a taxi when you can walk, expensive lunch.)

• Do you buy things you don't need?

• Are you overpaying for services such as auto insurance, cable TV, or cell phones?

• Do you have any unused memberships (e.g. gym memberships) that are still being paid for (and could be sold)?

They are easy to tell apart if you follow the textbook definition. But in reality, the distinction is complex, and over the past few years it has begun to narrow.

Today, despite the existence of efficient public transportation systems, cars have become an emotional necessity. Now the demand for cars has gone from being a status symbol to being a luxury and a necessity. The same logical system applies to food.

From homemade food to fast food restaurants, today's shoppers expect fine dining, not just delicious food. This atmosphere

Premium, people just don't mind paying for it.

The truth is that needs are limitless, and the boundaries between needs and wants are often blurred. So, before you spend money on motivation, you need to do some self-analysis.

Suppose a family of 4 spends $8,000 on food, $25,000 on housing, $20,000 on education, and $10,000 on transportation. Now calculate the difference between your expenses and income. All you need to do is write down the main price lists and cost of living in your city and compare these areas to get the real picture.

This is necessary if you need a phone due to field work. But if you insist on buying the latest gadget that you can actually afford, it's all too necessary. This is an easy choice. But if you have to change the washing machine for a refrigerator or a home theater-communications-music system instead of a radio, it's hard to think about it!

Chapter 3

Correct payment order

Once you adjust and optimize your budget, you will have a breather. What needs to be done first to free up money? The authorities are unanimous: even if you have debts, make savings a top priority.

Americans with a credit record have an average of $16,635 in debt, not counting mortgages. Suppose the deficit has an annual interest rate of 10%, and you pay $200 per month. If you owe nothing more, you will not be clean for twelve years.

The good news is that if you follow a few simple guidelines, you will be able to dig faster.

Once you break the habit of overspending and develop the habit of saving, you can move on to the next step: building investments, retirement savings, and real estate assets. Sounds impossible?

Change action

One of the oldest personal finance rules is a simple piece of advice: Pay yourself first. All books about money advise you to do this. All bloggers about personal finance talk about it. Even your parents gave you the same advice.

But it is difficult. Money can be used elsewhere. You can

pay your phone bills, pay off your debt, and buy a new video player. You've tried it once or twice in the past, but it's easy to forget. You don't have a budget, so when payday comes around, the income just goes elsewhere.

Paying yourself first means putting a portion of your income into savings before you pay your bills, buy food, or do anything else. Put income into your 401(k), Roth IRA, or savings account. The first bill you pay every month should be for you. Forming this habit early on can help you amass a large fortune.

Once you pay yourself first, you mentally make saving a priority. You tell yourself that you are more important than the lighting company or the homeowner. Savings is a powerful motivator—it empowers.

Paying yourself first will further develop good financial habits. Most people spend their money in this order: bills, entertainment, savings. No wonder there's not much left in the bank. But if you prioritize savings—savings, bills, entertainment—you can put off income until you can justify spending it.

By paying yourself first, you create a cash buffer for real applications. Stable contributions are a great way to accumulate savings. You can use this money to deal with emergencies. You can use it to buy a house. Furthermore, you can use it to save for retirement. Paying you first for freedom opens up a realm of possibilities.

The best way to develop the habit of saving money is to make the process as painless as possible. Do it automatically. Make it invisible. If you arrange to have the money deducted from your paycheck before you receive it, you'll never know it's gone.

The real roadblock to this habit is finding money to save. Many people think that this is impossible. But almost everyone can save at least 1% of their income. It's only one penny out of every dollar. Some will argue that saving on this is pointless. But if a skeptic tries to save as little as 1%, he usually finds the process painless. Maybe next time he will try to save 3%. Or 5%. As his savings rate increases, so does his savings.

If you're busy looking for money to save, consider saving your next raise for later. Set aside earnings for retirement and savings as your income grows. Once you've set a ceiling for your retirement (and created contingency savings), you can start using your increase for yourself again.

My friends,pay yourself first. This is a habit you will never regret.

If you already have a lot of credit card debt, start paying off the credit card with the highest interest rate first. Mathematically, this will save you the most interest. However, if you have a few small credit card balances, you may feel that paying them off individually first will make more progress.

Start keeping a close eye on your spending. To make ends meet, you may need to iron out some small issues in your budget. Restaurants, cinemas and other expensive entertainment venues could be replaced by libraries, galleries and outdoor sports facilities. Newspapers, magazine subscriptions, and cable TV are also great budget-saving options.

However, one expense that can be helpful is a personal financial plan that tracks your debts, assets, and cash flow on a daily basis, so you always know exactly where you are.

Whatever you do, never miss a payment. Late payments can seriously damage your credit score, making it harder for you to get more active funding. It may also affect your insurance rates. It is much better to pay the lower limit before your credit card expires than to pay a higher amount a few days later.

The second source of income can have a huge impact on debtors. If you can only earn $500 extra a month, you can apply for $6,000 a year debt relief. Another idea is to reduce the amount of tax you withhold on checks.

In some cases, it may be advantageous not to deduct taxes. Of course, you have to pay interest and penalties at the end of the year, but these rates are usually much lower than standard credit card rates.

If you need help, don't hesitate. Discuss terms with lenders to see if you can come up with a satisfactory solution. Credit and financial advisory services can be invaluable resources that can point you to options or advice you didn't even know existed.

They may also start managing your debt or a consolidation plan to lower your interest rates.

Finally, if all else fails, see if you can get a debt consolidation loan from a family member. You can pay them much lower interest rates than your credit card, but much higher rates than they would get on a checking or savings account.

Some investment steps to consider:

Meet with a financial advisor or certified financial planner to review all important parts of your budget.

Make a clear plan and stick to it. We often get complacent when the market is doing well, and we are cowardly when things are not going well. What distinguishes successful people is the inclusion of these emotions.

Why it's important:
Development personal and financial. You have to go from spender to economist, from economist to savor, from saver to investor.

Decide which projects or questions you want to keep. It could be retirement, a new home, your child's education, or whatever you choose.

Determine when you want to retire, buy a house, or send your kids to college to determine the percentage of return you need on your initial investment.

Determine how much to invest. Invest in what you can afford now, remembering that you can change this amount later.

Determine how much risk you are willing to take. Many investments offer high returns and are more risky than others.

Once you've decided how much you're willing to invest, how much you want to earn, when you need your money, and how much risk you're willing to take, you can build your portfolio.

An investment advisor or stockbroker is a good source of advice. Let these consultants know your goals and ask for their advice on how to distribute your income.

Reevaluate your portfolio at least once a year. Research every investment.

Chapter 4

Ways to save money

There are many ways to save money at home. On a day when you need to have fun, but your money is running out, you need to enjoy life! Believe it or not, the best things in life are free! Wherever you are, this content will show you how to have fun for free.

Some tricks

Save energy cost.

Insert new fluorescent tubes into lamps that you have left on for a long period of time. They give 4 times more light than incandescent bulbs and last 10 times longer. Possible savings: $10-50/year.

Lower the temperature of the water heater to 110-120 degrees. There is no need to make it hotter and waste energy. Potential savings: $20-40/year.

Find out if your utility company offers a free energy audit, they test your home's energy efficiency, and promote low-cost ways to reduce energy costs like insulated water heaters, seals, and more. Insulating your water heater alone can save you $25 a year. Potential savings: $50/year.

Set the thermostat to no higher than 68 degrees in winter and 78 degrees in summer. Turn off the heating at night or when you are not at home (unless you have a heat pump that works more efficiently at the same settings). The cost of heating can increase by 3% for every additional degree in winter. In summer, every degree can increase cooling costs by 6%. Potential Savings: $325 to $500 per year.

Reduce dryer usage. Not only does it consume a lot of energy, but it can quickly suck hot air out of your home in winter. Hang clothes on the dryer to dry, and then use the dryer to dry towels and other heavy items. Potential savings: $25-50/year.

If possible, use a microwave instead of an oven to save up to 50% on cooking energy. Potential savings: $50/year.

Saving income from water.

Always do a full wash. A typical full load uses about 21 gallons of water. Use 14 gallons for small loads. Several small loads use more water than one or two large loads. This adds up over the course of the year. Potential savings: $25-125/year.

Run the dishwasher only when it is fully loaded. Let the plate air dry instead of using a heat cycle. The average cost to operate a dishwasher is between $60 and $100 per year. Potential savings: $35-55/year.

A quick fix for a leaky toilet or leaky faucet. An infinity toilet can use over 8,000 gallons of water per year. Potential savings: $25-125/year.

Install a restrictive shower head. A family of four can save 8,000 to 12,000 gallons of water a year. You will save not only on water bills, but also on heating. Potential savings: $100-300/year.

Add fabric softener to your laundry at the appropriate time in the cycle rather than adding it at the end and run different rinse cycles that can use up to 10 gallons of water.

Calculate the time it takes your washing machine to complete a rinse cycle and set a timer so you can add softener at the right time. Potential savings: $25-100/year.

Wash clothes in warm or cold water and always rinse in cold water. Potential savings: $50/year.

Save money in other ways.

Use basic telephony. Additional services such as call waiting and call forwarding can nearly double your phone bill. Potential savings: $168/year.

If you can live without cables, you can save $300 to $600 a year. If you can't live without it, just get the basics. You can rent tons of movies for the extra $150-$600 a year you pay for movie channels like HBO, Showtime, and more. Potential savings: $144-700 per year.

Plant perennials instead of annuals. You get a one-time fee and enjoy flowers for a long time without much extra effort or income. On the other hand, yearbooks require an annual cost and effort. Potential savings: $100-300/year.

Go to the beach! The public beach is free and fun. You can also take a walk along the promenade. Have fun building sand castles or fishing on the pier.

Go window browsing. Go to the mall and check out what's new. Remember that you don't have to limit your window shopping to clothing stores. Stop at the windows of electronics and jewelry stores. Fresh tech gadgets are always on the market!

Ask about the company's free services. You may not know this, but often the company you work for has a list of free places (like museums and aquariums) that you can use for free if you show your work ID at the front desk!

Think of each season as a new way to have fun. In summer, you can play basketball on the basketball court, play tennis or take a walk nearby with friends. In autumn, you can take your camera and take pictures of the autumn leaves. Fall is also a great time to head to the pumpkin patch. It's fun in the winter because you can play in the snow or stay home and watch the snow with hot chocolate or a latte. Spring is good for cycling!

Invite your friends over for an evening of board games, cards, and anagrams. The bonus is the choice of side dish or drink. Your donation will be free entertainment, so be prepared to accept!

Stay at home with the youth? Whether they're coming home from school or on the weekend, here are some great tips to keep them entertained for free.

Consider going to free community festivals, free movie screenings, and free parks.

Think about a day at the beach, a picnic in the park, a hike in the woods, or some other outdoor activity. Swimming, outdoor play and adventure are all affordable and effective ways to spend a day with your kids.

Also prepare a list of ideas to plan ahead. Visit the local library, rent some movies for the kids and play "cinema": ask the kids to recoup their tickets, set up the living room as a movie theater and popcorn. You can also make your own novelty board games around the house, draw and color games, or make simple crafts.

Take advantage of upgrades. It may cost more at first, but consider year-round passes to local attractions a great way to spend the day. Your local zoo or aquarium may offer such offerings, as well as playgrounds and more.

In general, children have ideas about the capital! Just be prepared to give them a free or affordable option. For example, if they suggest going for ice cream, consider buying ice cream and cones at the food market and heading to the park. If they want to go for pizza pie, buy the ingredients to make the pizza, or turn it into an activity. Having a good imagination and a willingness to try new things will help you go further and increase your bankroll while entertaining the youth.

Chapter 5

Bring extra cash with tech skills

Everyone has a balance of money to use, especially during difficult times. Maybe this month's bill is a little bigger than you expected, or you're trying to raise start-up capital for your own online startup or business, or you just need to figure out how to grow an existing business.

Make an e-book: Well, you must be - everyone and his father are doing it now. However, why? Because it works. If you're good at topics like ventilating your patio, cleaning your house, quitting smoking, making doll costumes—whatever it is, write a book about it.

A bit more

Freelancers are a group of dreamers. However, almost every day I get questions from people who are struggling to lead a stable life. I attribute much of this to some people's inability to think differently.

As a freelancer, there are many ways to make money, and I've put those thoughts on the record. Although I'm rarely without a project on my desk when things get scarce, I use this file to revitalize my brain cells. Today I will share my thoughts with you.

This may require some upfront work, but can bring in

dollars over a long period of time. With so many websites in desperate need of a great copy, all you have to do is turn on your computer to open one. However, the point is to target those who are willing to pay you for your services.

My friend knows a pharmacist who makes skin care products. Products are sold throughout the country through independent distributors. A friend of mine advised me to check the site to see if it was a product that I would be interested in trying.

When I got to the site, I immediately forgot why I need to check it. how did it get here? The syntax, typography and layout are terrible, especially the syntax! I rewrote the main page and sent it to the webmaster with a polite note that I would be happy to remake the whole site for $ x. A few days later we made a deal and I got the job. You can do it too.

Professionals are a good target market for freelancers. Mortgage companies, insurance companies, lawn care providers and more. Most have websites, many of which are not very good. So edit/rewrite the page and send them an offer to complete the entire site.

Usually, if they use you once, they will continue to do so for years. Offers weekly, monthly, quarterly, etc. additions. Add articles to your site to increase traffic. Many small business owners are too busy to think or understand how to do this type of marketing. Pay attention to your strengths and watch your client list grow.

Consider the content of each page. For example, you can enter the history of the company on the About Us page, but you can also indicate on the main page that your company has x years of experience. You can list your services on the main page and learn more about them on the Services page. Write down a few points for the content of each page. Decide where you want to highlight certain tidbits, so they don't repeat themselves on every page.

Add some SEO. Do a little research online to determine which keywords are hot in the industry. For example, if a company manufactures kitchen cabinets, you might include terms such as "kitchen remodel", "kitchen cabinets", and "kitchen cabinets". It is also a good idea to provide regional information for those looking to do business locally. For example, "Arizona kitchen cabinet manufacturer" and "Arizona kitchen cabinet" are good copy words.

Use a catchy title for every page. Instead of "cabinetmaker" you could try something like "unique custom kitchen cabinets". When you get to the "base" don't forget to talk to your assigned audience.

Do you represent clients directly? Nobody cares about content if it doesn't give them something. Rather than brag about why a company is the best or show off the history of kitchen cabinets, it's helpful to remember that you need to explain the benefits of what the company has to offer. What does Joe Blow get from the site, and why did he choose this company to make his cabinets?

I always end each page with a simple call to action. For example, "Are you ready to learn how to make the kitchen of your dreams? Please contact us by (telephone) or e-mail (e-mail)." The goal is to encourage the reader to take action.

Creating an e-book is easy - it can be done in as little as 24 hours - and you can sell it on sites like Click Bank or Commission Junction. But think about it, most people look for information online. In addition, "how to" information is one of the most popular forms.

So, brainstorm what you love to do, write an e-book about it, and sell it through major distributors like Click Bank. The book may not make you rich, but it can bring in extra money for a long time. The most beneficial part of this idea is that by making one e-book, you can make other e-books and really increase your income until you quit your crappy day job.

Think about your target audience, your book's strengths for them, its essence, and focus like a laser on that. It seems to you that only everyone wants to read your book, but such thinking can make your book too "general". Remember that if you focus your efforts on specific topics rather than generalizations, you will effectively reach a specific audience and get more potential sales. It's like centering a puddle instead of an ocean.

Know your target audience, what problem can your book solve for them? Where is your book buying audience? Try to create a headline that includes your audience. If not, maybe in the subtitle?

You must be the author and promoter, so when you create your book, write about it and make up your sales pitch. Gather data about yourself for your author profile (if you qualify to write a book and possibly other publishing credits, any experience is a plus), write down what your potential buyers are looking for, and perhaps you have the benefits found in the book. Get multiple referrals.

Visit places like Amazon to see which books sell well and read their "fuzzy" content on how to present your thoughts. It's also a good idea to visit a local bookstore. Check out some other online marketing books for marketers. Search for "e-book". How are they sold?

Create an attractive table of contents for your book. Give your chapter a title and add a subtitle, so your readers can understand what it contains. Read other authors' TOCs to get an idea of what might "grab attention".
This should get you going. Now do an internet search and find the information you need to get started, but beware of blackmailers trying to swindle you out of your money. Subscribe to some legitimate people's newsletters. Think about each step of the process, take notes, and move on.

Chapter 6

Creative ways to make money

Places like CafePress.com or zazzle.com allow you to make t-shirts, mugs, stickers and more and sell them without having to carry any stock. There is no floor, no inventory, no prepayment. If you're not selling anything, you don't have to pay anything.

It's a bit tricky, but once applied, it can really attract a bunch of buyers! Again, I would target the professional market.
Well, not glamorous. However, it can be lucrative and a never-ending need. The great thing about resume writing is that if you don't like it or don't have the time to invest, it's an easily developed and outsourced part of your business.
Innovation
So how can freelancers make the most of creative media? Simply put, if you have a strong pen, the dollar can follow you. Create cool slogans and humorous sayings and put them on t-shirts, stickers, mugs and more. You can be the creator of the next pandemic t-shirt. Think of the motto "Shit happens?" I think it was popular with florists in the seventies. Can you even guess how many bumper stickers and t-shirts are sold with this one? So strain your brain and

create some fantastic pop culture!

T-shirts come in a variety of styles and colors. Are you targeting a female audience? One of the many t-shirts you can consider for women - dolls, vests, thin shoulder straps and more. Pay attention to the color of your shirt. While the colors are attractive, they can also clash or overwhelm each other. Make sure the colors you choose—the t-shirt itself, any printed information, and the colors of any graphics—will work together to create your canvas. You want the color of the shirt to complement or contrast with the design. Keep in mind that pink letters may not show up well on a pink shirt if the two pinks are too similar.

There is something to "declare" the world. Effective information articulates this in a memorable way. Think of those timeless slogans, simple combinations of words that most people have heard. Your job as a T-shirt designer is to come up with new slogans, mottos or catchphrases. Short ones are usually better because they are easier to remember. But even a longer message can be memorable if it flows and has a beat or rhythm.

Try different fonts. When choosing a font, remember that legibility is important. But there is also the visual aspect. Choose a font that will add depth to your message. For example, if the message is "Work makes me crazy," the font might be scribbled or look crazy, but still be legible. Ideally, you will design in a graphics program such as Photoshop and then use your images on a website.

Consider art. Draw/make art to express feelings. What emotion do you want to evoke? Identify elements of the image that naturally elicit the desired response, and then emphasize those elements. Are you trying to find a sense of beauty or fear in those who see your designs? The key is to understand the parts of the artwork and build on them. Arrange art and text so that they do not distract each other. Art can stand behind the text—if the art itself isn't too busy. Art can be above or below text. This works especially well with an oval image, so the image is mostly highlighted or placed on top of a line of text. Your art can also run down the sides of the t-shirt, or even cross over from front to back.

If you are using Photoshop or a similar application, scan and import the art image into your file. Including art can enhance your message. If the vision is the message you want to convey, or use only art.

 Ads

Example: There is a very famous land agent in my city. In all my years, I have never seen an agency with such a specific advertising model. He prepared a "dissertation" about his geographical area. It has only five or six pages (11x17), and it was published in a newspaper. It has all the local events, what is being built, how it will affect the biological community, and so on. Of course, this article is focused on real estate news, but there are enough additional factors to attract loyal regular readers. In this article, he provides advertising to mortgage brokers, movers, ownership and lending companies, car dealers, etc. Now, when people go to sell a house, who do you think they will call? He, of course! Since his name was in their sight, he brought them news related to their daily lives over and over again.

It is very important for you to understand everything about the dissertation. If you are a beginner and make a cold call, you will get questions about your publication. If you can answer them correctly, you will build trust in your vision.

If you make a mistake and cannot provide reliable information, you will have a hard time.

You should be familiar with your price and the size of each advertisement put up for sale. Ads can be sold by column inches or pages, and pages are subdivided into certain sizes, such as full pages, half pages, 1/4 pages, etc. It is very important that you can fully detect ads and distinguish their size. Save this information in memory.

List the businessmen you know. Start calling to set up sales. If you're new to sales advertising games, it's safe to assume that you don't have an existing business book. This, of course, does not mean that you will not be able to start selling. Almost everyone knows a person who holds a managerial position or owns a business. This is your fast market.

It is important for you to create a sense of urgency among your potential customers. However, do not rush to success. No one likes to be pressured. However, keep in mind that you are not selling physical goods such as cars or copiers. Your task is to promote the "concept" of advertising.

Sold from top to bottom. This step is very important. Regardless of your potential customers' budget, show them your biggest and most expensive ads first. They may only think about a little advertising, but they may not realize that by spending a little more money, they will use their advertising dollars more wisely.

Become a master. You'll find that after the first few months, most of your sales will come from follow-ups. Even experienced professionals won't sell on the first try. You should be examined no later than 3-5 days after the first contact. After eight or ten unsuccessful attempts to close a potential buyer, move on to another buyer. Your time is too precious to waste on those who are not ready to buy.

Resume

At an ultra-low price of $50 (the price of my quoted resume is $250); just doing a couple of tasks a day can bring in a very good full-time income. It is usually very easy to sell a package (for example, a cover letter and a reference sheet), and the customer is very grateful that this feeling is enough to make it worthwhile.

The most difficult thing in writing a resume is to know what to focus on. You should attract the attention of HR managers who receive more than 100 resumes every day, even if they do not announce any vacancies.

Write a cover letter. This is not a summary of your resume. Just introduce yourself and explain why you are the best candidate for this job.

Understand the type of job and the qualifications you are applying for.

Choose the design of your resume. You can search for samples specific to the job you are applying for, although it is more important to have a scheme that is most suitable for this job and fill in the gaps with personal information. The plan may include goals, work experience, qualifications, and reference materials.

Specify the goal in the resume and match the job description. This can determine whether a person will receive a review lasting 10 to 30 seconds and whether the reviewer will send your resume to the next round.

Use key points to convey information, and strive for clarity and brevity when writing the rest of your resume. Analyze the job qualifications and highlight any skills that meet these requirements. It is also the best use of action words such as preparation, leadership, management, development, supervision, implementation, coordination and remuneration. If you lack experience, please pay attention to how education prepares them for the position they are applying for.

Includes characters such as %, $, and #. These symbols will save space and allow you to include more information in your resume. Symbols such as the dollar sign can also attract the attention of HR managers to achieve major financial achievements. For example, "The first year of orientation and closure with an income of $2 million" should be replaced with "the first year of orientation and closure with an income of $22 million"."

Highlight the benefits by placing the most relevant points of view where they can be quickly viewed. Maintain a positive attitude and prevent negative factors, such as the reason for leaving the employer and the historical gap in employment. If necessary, you can discuss these issues in person.

Helping students

Ah, the charming, bankrupt, desperate teacher. Many of them don't have the time or, frankly, the skill level to edit their own work. Moreover, they will be happy to pay someone for it.

This is one of the easiest markets to target because all you have to do is contact the Student Affairs department and ask them to post a notice on the student bulletin board. Or you can advertise in the university newspaper. In addition, the flyers posted all over the campus are very effective.

Usually, if a student uses you once, if he is satisfied with your service, he will always return. What is the best thing about this group of people? They have loud voices, and they use them - tell other students about your services.

Students also need resumes, bibliographies and theses. You can successfully provide many services. I can tell you from personal experience that they are paid very well and cooperate very well - because they are usually desperate and just happy to find someone who can work on time (think: "I needed this yesterday!").

I do not recommend writing an essay directly for students. I think it's unethical. Nevertheless, proofreading, editing, suggestive changes are the services that I have provided quite successfully in the past.

Chapter 7

Payment card and borrowing

When people first decided to start accumulating wealth and using their income for the future, one of the biggest problems they had to overcome was the huge credit card debt that had accumulated over the years. Debt should come first.

In addition, many financial planners will advise you to use a HELOC, or home equity line of credit, to pay off high-interest credit card debt. Don't do that.

Viewing debt

Do you prefer to know that someone is not ready to take responsibility for their financial life and be responsible for credit card debt in the fastest way? It's that they still blame other people, the economy, the economic system, the form of government, their boss or anyone else.

The only reasonable and logical excuses are those unhappy people who find themselves in a terrible panic about their health and are burdened with huge debts for this. If it's not you, you need to find something: cut it off.

You're not a nasty person. You are not a stupid person. You just made some stupid decisions. It has nothing to do with your income. It has nothing to do with the person you love. Every time you use your paid card, you consciously decide to borrow something that you don't have. In the first month, an extract appeared. You cannot repay the total balance in full. You have exceeded your resources. This is the moment when you are in trouble.

This topic should not upset! On the contrary, it should give you strength. If you are mired in a huge credit card debt, then you have the opportunity to get rid of it. It's so simple. The moment you can look in the mirror and say "It's my fault" and sincerely accept the situation, you can start to change the situation like 1,000,000 people.

Get your strength back. Discover the symbol of your inner feelings or self-confidence that you want to show to others. Having a symbol of what you think or work hard is the key to gaining confidence. To get to the finish line or achieve any goals, you need to know where you are going. Your symbol can be any color that makes you feel strong, or an event in your life that really makes you feel strong.

Make a contract with yourself and always put yourself first. The struggle for self-confidence often goes downhill because people tend to put the needs of others above their own. If you really want to gain any advantage in your life, you need to put yourself first.

If you want to learn the real secret of how to gain credibility, try your best every day. It's a fact that shows that those who put on what they think is their best costume and do their hair and makeup in a way as if they're going out on a special evening in the city feel more powerful. I bet you don't know that the simple task of putting on a shirt saved for "special occasions" in your daily life will help you get more guarantees than any self-help master.

Regain your strength and take responsibility.

A few of my friends have a lot of credit card debt, and they sometimes ask me how to get rid of the status quo. While I'm happy to take the time to help them, 90% of the time it's almost always a pointless activity, and people aren't very serious about getting rid of credit card debt. Of course, they are in pain because of the payment, and most of all they want their credit card account to have a balance of $100. Wanting something and doing something to actively own it are two completely different things.

The person I know (I'll call Tom) earns about $85,000 a year and has $20,000 in credit card debt. This debt spread like a plague, and he had to be nervous for several hours every day to pay more than $500 a month in interest to maintain his current balance. However, in any case, once a month he found $100 for weekend trips. When I asked him about it, he said that no matter how big the debt is, he will never give up something special.

Tom may never get rid of his credit card debt with such a mental attitude. The additional $1,200 he spends every year on weekends will allow him to pay the principal amount of $6,000, or almost 40% of the balance, over 5 years. If he can earn an extra 50 yen a week by working long hours or cutting costs (yes, that actually means you ride a bike, not driving), he can pay an extra 11,000 yen for those 5 years. That's all it takes to eliminate the balance.

On the contrary, he thinks about "my vacation money" or "my money at the food market." No, you have a lot of money at your disposal. If you are responsible for credit card debt, pay huge interest on your balance, take every extra penny you can and pay off the debt.

Set a monthly amount for food, water and shelter, because these are your basic needs. You need to think about buying a variety of healthy foods and try to avoid unnecessary snacks. You also need to do your best at work because it's your source of income to pay the bills. This is where you start setting your priorities right.

Some people confuse their priorities and even ignore their health in order to buy expensive gadgets or travel. Remember that taking care of your daily needs is your responsibility and priority, so don't put off important things, especially if you have a family.

Pay off your credit card debt. Paying off a credit card with the highest interest rate and then paying off a credit card with a lower interest rate is the most profitable thing you can do to pay off your credit card debt in full. Use as much cash as possible to buy things and control your expenses.

Also save enough money for your emergency fund. This is very important in case of unemployment or other serious unforeseen circumstances that may happen to you. Avoid the temptation to buy things you can live without and focus on accumulating savings in case of unforeseen circumstances.

Adjusting your financial priorities should be your biggest concern. There is a clear list that will cover your monthly payments and financial situation, and will number each item from the highest to the lowest according to its importance and needs.

For a simple reason, I'm not a big fan of the home equity line – if you decide to use the nuclear option and declare bankruptcy, your payment card balance is not guaranteed, and the home equity credit line is guaranteed by your home.

In fact, this means that you have taken on a debt that is supported only by your credit. The worst thing a company providing paid cards can do is go to court and make a decision against you, enter your house to pay off the debt, and the worst is even worse – the bank can cancel your loan. House and kick you out.

In any case, this is entirely your decision, because it will come down to something that will allow you to rest at night. If your credit card debt is manageable, and you just want to save a few thousand dollars on interest charges, an equity line of credit may arise. If you think there is even a remote possibility that you may be forced to declare bankruptcy, it could be a tragic mistake that will cost you your home.

There are a lot of loan lenders out there today who want you to take equity in your home to get your money for almost any reason you can be sure of. The ways you can get equity from your lender include refinancing, getting a second mortgage, an equity loan, and an equity line of credit. Is it a good idea to use these methods to borrow money to reduce debt? Here are some good reasons why you shouldn't use equity in your home to pay off debts:

If you have financial problems, and you feel that you will have to default on a new secured debt, the new debtor can file a foreclosure claim to get the money because the house is secured with interest. Lenders of unsecured loans, such as commission cards, cannot cancel their mortgages because their loans are not guaranteed by equity.

Even in a few areas where the market is falling, your home can rise in value. This means that your assets will increase over time. When you borrow against your own equity to pay off the debt, you will lose the accumulated value of the house if your house is foreclosed on. Not only will you owe the amount of the guaranteed loan, but in many cases, the sale of the foreclosed property will cost cents in US dollars. Thus, the equity capital, which, according to your forecasts, will be used to repay new guaranteed loans, will not be enough to repay them.

Getting into debt seems to be a symptom of a deeper problem. Using your assets to pay off debts does not guarantee that new debts will not arise. If a new debt arises, you have liquidated your only asset, it already belongs to someone else, and you have increased your debt burden to a level that you may not be able to afford.

Chapter 8

Financial control skills

You can sell assets. If the interest rate you pay exceeds 10-12% and is tax-free, then reducing your debt level is almost always the best choice.

Another strategy is the snowball strategy, which can help you deal with credit card debt and pay off your balance with high interest rates much faster than you can take advantage of the random payment system.

The Snowflake strategy is designed to help you pay off your credit card debt by sending so-called micropayments. These payments can actually be several dollars, and over time they will significantly reduce the balance, saving you thousands of dollars in interest charges.

Intelligent technology

If you have any investments, you can sell them and pay off the balance on your payment card. However, you really have to be careful with the ones you sell, because if you make a risky choice, there could be very terrible tax consequences.

Think about 401(k) loans to pay off credit card debt:

You will be able to treat 401(k) loans in the same way, because the interest you pay will flow into your account (in fact, you pay the interest for yourself). The bottom line is that as long as you repay the loan within the time allowed by the IRS, you can avoid income tax and a 10% penalty for early withdrawals. In most cases, you won't just want to sell 401(k) assets, cash them out and pay off your credit card debt.

You can withdraw contributions from your individual Roth retirement account:

The IRS rules allow you to withdraw contributions from your individual retirement account that you have deposited into your account, but you cannot withdraw income from that money. In other words, if you have deposited 20,000 yen into an individual Roth retirement account over the past ten years and earned 10,000 yen in income, then you can withdraw an amount equivalent to 20,000 yen without adverse tax penalties or consequences (of course, you have lost decades of time to develop your money in your hands about Uncle Sam, but this is much better than drowning in high-interest credit card debt).

Brokerage company and additional investment account:

Investments that you hold in regular brokerage accounts, such as stocks and bonds, will be subject to a stable capital gains tax, but when you notice that most of your payment card debt is falling, the emotional release should be more painless than the reduction taken by the IRS.

The goal of being responsible for your financial life is to increase your cash flow every month. The more extra money you have, the more you need to reduce debts or spend on improving your lifestyle.

Each debt has a lower limit of monthly payments. First, after paying off the lower balance on the payment card account, you withdraw the entire fixed payment and immediately replenish your existing funds.

Then you take the income from the credit card debt balance with the lowest payment you pay and send it to the most modest account below. You repeat this process until you leave your only, the heaviest debt.

In the financial planning industry, this approach is called a "snowball" because you send a little amount of money to each payment snowball, because each debt is reduced until you send a lot of cash to cover your biggest and last debt.

The one who has a balance of 10,000 on the Bank of America payment card, 3000 on the department store payment card and 1000 on the gas station payment card will send all the additional money to the filling station card filling1 000.

As soon as this debt is cancelled, they will take all the paid income and blow up the department store card worth 3,000 yen. This cycle repeats until all debts are repaid. This is a really effective way to reduce and pay off credit card debt, and it's easy to understand.

Paid card: We love them, we hate them, don't we? Paid cards can make your life easier - or really complicate it! You can learn how to make the most of your charging card and how to avoid the pitfalls associated with a charging card.

You've just discovered a "snowball" strategy for reducing credit card debt, so it's time to talk about the so-called "snowflake" strategy. The premise is simple: every time you have more than a few dollars on hand, send them to the company issuing your credit card to reduce the balance of your debt.

To make it clear: in fact, we are talking about a payment of 7.15 yen. Or pays14.50 payment. Or payments3.20

payment. If you leave them in the bank, you will spend them. This is human nature. If you can get an extra $2.74 a day, it will be deducted from the amount owed on your credit card every year!

Individuals often ignore a small amount of power. As with everything in life, there is a complex effect. This is the same principle that underlies the Indian story about ants being able to move an entire mountain, a grain of sand and a little soil at a time.

It may seem that your small efforts are not reducing credit card debt. In general, in a few years the result will be nothing short of outstanding. This is the essence of the universe.

Multiple payments are possible:

Coordinate salary checks and payments more carefully. Do you have a weekly salary? Pay a small amount of money every week instead of a large amount of money every month. You will balance your monthly cash flow.

Pay off your credit card debts faster, just like you pay off your mortgage every two weeks. With a mortgage every two weeks, the homeowner pays half of the mortgage amount every month, but they pay every 2 weeks. There are fifty-two weeks in a year, which means twenty-six and a half payments - or thirteen monthly payments instead of 12. As for mortgage loans, payments every two weeks can shorten the term of a 30-year mortgage by 7 years. If you split your monthly payment into 2 parts and then pay every two weeks, the same rules will apply.

Take advantage of the unexpected profit. Once you get into the habit of making multiple payments, if there are any unforeseen expenses in your wallet, you will think about credit card payments.

Develop good payment habits and increase satisfaction. Watching your balance drop day by day allows you to focus on the task of getting out of debt and develop a sense of accomplishment.

Chapter 9

Other ways to get out of debt

One of the strategies proposed by financial planners to reduce payment card debt is to freeze your card in the form of ice cubes, which will help you avoid the temptation to make non-essential purchases.

Find a way to make some extra money.
In the field of personal finance, the atomic version of the "big red button" went bankrupt.
Dig it out
A long time ago, a financial planner advised customers to freeze their payment cards in ice cubes. When they are tempted to spend money, they are forced to melt the ice, which gives them time to think about impulse purchases again.
A better answer is to cut your card completely so that you can't charge them any other fees. If you keep drilling new holes by the boat, what's the point of plugging holes in your boat?
Some people may be thinking... But I can't pay the bill without a payment card! This means I can't eat.
This may sound cruel, but I have news for you: you didn't actually pay the bill. The payment card just allows you to

postpone the beginning of the moment of destiny and helps to ensure that when it comes, everything will be much worse than you thought.

If you are right, you are almost certainly eligible for free food assistance in your state (if you don't, move to the state you do—I'm serious). In several states, you can get up to three to four hundred dollars a month in the form of tax-free food money on your debit card. If you do not meet the requirements, it means that you have a problem with the fee, and you are still giving a reason (back to Chapter 1).

If you still claim that you can't give credit: you are really full of it. I apologize again, but this is straightforward.

When I was young, I moved to another state to pay half of my monthly rent of one hundred and eighty dollars for the apartment I shared with my best friend. At the time, I received a six-figure income from my investment portfolio and had almost no debt. At that time, my goal was to accumulate my wealth. Are you happy? Maybe not quite. However, what I want is what few people achieve- complete financial independence.

I have a family member who slept on an air cushion for a year and a half in order to save more than $40,000 when he retired from the Marine Corps at the age of 25. If I can do it, and he can do it, then there is absolutely no reason why you can't do it. Make up your mind to achieve what you want and keep credit cards out of reach.

I know someone who decides that he wants to get out of debt. She decided that within a year, she would completely take back everything that happened in her life until the gorgeous new car she recently purchased.

In addition to her daily work, she also found a job as a bartender, saved every penny after tax, and used it to repay the outstanding balance in her account. She temporarily suspended all investments, including retirement stocks, to achieve the goals she thought she should achieve.

What she has achieved in a short period of time is absolutely amazing. Six months later, it seems that she can easily achieve her goal. By adding more money to the equation, she was able to combine the savings from regular work (she also gave up her mobile phone, cable TV, and many other unnecessary items) to achieve a double effect.

Once this voluntary financial diet is over, her monthly income will increase by as much as a few thousand dollars without an extra working hour. In fact, she increased her salary. Despite raising her children and working two jobs, she recently entered the university and went back to get her degree.

The meaning of this story is very important. If you focus on yourself and are willing to make the necessary sacrifices to achieve this goal, then there is absolutely nothing you cannot achieve. In her case, this will mean working around the clock for a year to ensure new balance sheets and more profitable employment opportunities. I am willing to bet that in many years, she will look back and realize that it was these twelve months that allowed her to realize her big goals and dreams, including creating her own business.

As the old saying goes, until the pain of staying the same exceeds the pain of changing, you are unlikely to give in. I hope you don't need this to gain strength and free yourself from financial slavery.

Companies that issue payment cards, many of which are owned by banks, have many priorities. Of course, the first is to bring profits to the parent company and its shareholders (in fact, you can become a shareholder through the mutual funds you hold in your 401(k) account without even realizing it).

When it is obvious that someone may not be able to pay their balance, there is a change in priority that can benefit you. The bank or company that issues the payment card only cares about one issue: get as much money as possible from your balance and close or restrict your account. How did this happen? This allows them to avoid writing off the amount in the income statement, which will lead to a decline in their stocks, a decrease in management bonuses, and possibly even a decrease in dividends paid to shareholders.

If you declare bankruptcy, it is very likely that the entire credit balance will be destroyed, because in most cases, the debt on the payment card is called unsecured. This means that it does not have any specific commitment to support, only your commitment to repay the debt. For payment card companies, this will be the worst case scenario.

If you have missed a lot of payments and your credit score has dropped, all you need is a series of calls to the company explaining that you are seriously considering bankruptcy, but want to avoid it. You want to pay off as much debt as you can, but honestly, you don't know if it is possible. Then offer to pay off 25% of the payment card debt within the next few months in exchange for the company freezing interest charges and closing the account.

It may take you hours or even days to talk on the phone to figure out the system. The bottom line is that you need to remember a concept: you are on the verge of declaring bankruptcy, but you would rather avoid it at all costs. Tell them you are taking out a loan from your relatives, or cashing in your 401(k), or any other story you need to come up with to convince them that you are doing everything you might be able to do, which is what they hope. If you can convince them of this, you have a good chance to reach an agreement to resolve credit card debt.

Settlement agreements to pay card debts come with serious costs, which are manifested in the form of extremely poor credit scores. However, if you have missed the payment, it is unlikely to cause any additional damage in a practical sense, because you will not find someone willing to lend you overdue payments–at least at a fair interest rate, anyway.

The bottom line is that a payment card debt settlement agreement can be an effective way for you to avoid bankruptcy court, the company issues a payment card to return some of their money, and for both parties to start repairing their balance sheets and income statements. If you really want to control your financial situation, then the biggest thing that prevents you from thinking about it may be pride. Not worth it. Accept it, accept the temporary pain, and start to get your financial life back on track. There is a significant minority of Americans who live without credit card debt-there is no reason why you can't be among them.

As a last resort... There is bankruptcy:

In many cases, you can pay off your credit card debt in full by filing for bankruptcy, or at least restructure your debt through a court order, which will give you a break to pay off the balance and keep your life in order. The alternative price for such a step is that your loan will be completely destroyed for up to 10 years, and most of the legal losses will be repaid after 7 years.

For some people, bankruptcy is indeed the best and most effective alternative to getting rid of payment card debt. This allows you to start over, almost like pressing the reset button in a computer game. One disadvantage to consider is that the bankruptcy rules introduced by the payment card lobby during the Bush administration may force many middle-class or working-class workers to apply for Chapter 13 (reorganization, in which you repay the debt from future net income) instead of Chapter 7 (liquidation, the debt is fully repaid). The U.S. Congress is currently enacting laws to change this, and some changes have already occurred.

Chapter 10

Real estate

Making money in real estate has always been a topic for those who want to invest. This includes many different types of real estate investment. Land, apartment buildings, residential buildings, and commercial buildings are all part of real estate investment.

Real estate/Real Property
Distribution of contracts: In the circle of real estate agents, the distribution of contracts is often called "wholesale". Think about how other large companies sell goods in bulk to make a profit. For example, Walmart sells goods in bulk and buys in large quantities. Because their purchasing power is too high, they may buy products that are much lower than the current market value. Walmart then turned around and sold these products to end customers at retail prices. Walmart can generate net profit by collecting the difference between the sales price of the product and the purchase price.
In fact, there are only three main steps in this process.

Discuss the conditions for obtaining product discounts.
This product is sold at retail price.

Do this within an effective time frame to minimize inventory.

There are several similar laws and several different laws for wholesale real estate. When selling wholesale real estate, you can also negotiate a reduction in the price of the product, and you can also sell this product (real estate) at a retail price. The main deviation is that you don't have any stocks, and you didn't negotiate a price reduction by buying in large quantities.

Justice: You may or may not be familiar with this term. Equity is the deviation of the value of the property minus the amount owed by the property. The seller owes the first mortgage of the house 75,000 and the second mortgage 25,000, which is estimated to be about 13,000. How much equity is there in the house? Equity = cost overdue debt= $130,000 - $75,000 - $25,000 = Example: $ 30,000 equity in the house.

How to accumulate equity? For anyone who owns a house, they can usually accumulate equity in any collateral way.

1) First payment.

2) Pay off the mortgage over time.

3) The value of real estate is growing.

4) Home decoration or decoration.

Why consider equity? It is very rare to sell a property at a much higher price than the market price. Real estate has a largely standardized value in the local market anywhere in the world. If the house next door to you sells for$100,000, it is extremely unlikely that the house will sell for$200,000 without any changes in the market or the property itself. There are many original ways to get a lot of money in real estate. However, they all focus on this simple and most importantly, basic commandment. You negotiate to participate in shares, and then sell your capital.

On the other hand, in some other initial investment strategies, you negotiate a low monthly payment and then sell your monthly payment at the market price.

So what is wholesale real estate? Wholesale real estate is a discussion of the discount terms of real estate objects. It is possible to sign a contract and then sell the real estate object to another investor at a price close to the market price at the same time. Since you sell the property at the same time, the final buyer will provide the necessary capital and credit to complete the transaction. In addition, since the contract can be terminated, if you cannot find a qualified final buyer who will purchase your capital, you can withdraw from your sale and purchase agreement. You will only buy properties that you have already sold with net profit.

It shouldn't surprise you that real estate has spawned more millionaires than any other type of business. There are dozens of advertisements talking about investing in real estate "without investment". Is there really a "no investment" real estate investment? Without any real estate skills or experience, can people really get rich?

In short, yes, but it depends a lot on you. I mean, if I don't know your skills, motivation and aspirations, how can I really make a commitment to you openly? What I want to show you are the strategies that can ensure a high-income life. What you do with these strategies is your choice.

Believe it or not, this kind of material is the kind of real estate that most people invest 5,000 in for beginners in seminars of other masters.

So is it possible to make a lot of money in real estate? The problem is, if you are willing to work hard, then yes, it can be done. When people think that this is a "get rich quick" strategy, wrong thinking occurs. In fact, a lot of income can be obtained quickly, but this requires reasonable targeted actions using proven strategies. If I say I don't need to work, I'm lying. Investing in real estate without investment is more like a topic of "getting rich slowly". If you apply the right strategies and methods, this can work quickly. You also need to maximize your efficiency to complete this operation in a short time, but this is entirely possible. If you believe that you can do very little and make a fortune without working, then this is not for you. I just don't want you to have empty expectations of what you can actually do in real life. If you don't plan to do anything to get the money, I will advocate the lottery. Otherwise, buy a repeatable system that can be automated over time to bring stable income and provide you with a better life.

However, having said that, there is a way to do it, and the good news is that I will show you how to do it. After all, it is no coincidence that studies have repeatedly shown that more than 9 out of 10 millionaires can directly attribute their wealth to real estate.

Contract allocation is the easiest way for beginners to start investing. Since investment does not require funds, even experienced real estate professionals often use this method. I know several experienced investors who have done a good job for themselves, and they are making full use of this strategy to gain their wealth. If you can shop without cash, hey, why don't you quit, right?

Why doesn't everyone do this? Because so many masters have made false promises and comments.

You need real expectations, what are the requirements for you in the real world. If you are diligent in your efforts, the strategy does work. Let's take a look at Question #1, I always hear it. After people see the logic behind the strategy, they inevitably ask the question: "Then why doesn't everyone do this?"" If you are like most people, then at some point you will believe the same thing, if you haven't believed it yet. Most people doubt themselves and are too afraid to try. They will even tell you that it will not work for you. Many people even mentally prevent themselves from attracting a lot of money, because in their minds, they think they are poor, so it is difficult for them to perform actions that lead to a lot of wealth. They may even bring themselves to such an extent that they are completely afraid to take action. If not, they want it to be really simple, just because they know some strategies.

They usually don't have any clear goals or strategic guidelines to guarantee their victory. But the biggest reason, despite this, has always been the attention to rejection. They can't get rid of the idea that another person might say no, so they will continue to live a life based on what other people tell them to do.

The problem is, if you have thought about it, you are already aware of it. The sad fact is that most people spend more time planning their vacations than taking responsibility for their finances. The real estate did not refuse. In real estate, you will always keep in touch with people who are interested in selling the house to you in advance, so you will never "refuse" in this way. The "rejection" in real estate sounds like this: "Oh, well, we won't do such a thing now" from the seller. You will answer questions like this: "Okay, thank you, good luck, if your conditions change, please feel free to call me." However, know that the fear of rejection will still guide many people.

This is one of the most important life lessons I can give you. Getting reasonable investment advice means always paying attention to the advice you are receiving. In the past, those who most often discouraged you from leaving great ideas were those who knew them the least. This is unfortunate because they are often your friends or parents. They have good suggestions on many issues, but they are not always ideas related to getting rich. If you need investment advice, find a good investor. Investment advice can only come from successful investors. If a successful investor tells you not to do something, you should listen to him. Otherwise, learn to disconnect from those who don't know anything about what you are doing. In short, never accept complex advice from people who are not familiar with this area.

Wrapping Up

If good habits are not formed, success will fail. It definitely helps people to support themselves in achieving their goals, because it promotes the development of good habits along the way so that the goals remain "alive". Create and maintain good habits with daily affirmations to ensure success for individuals and goals.

In the pursuit of goals, numerous failures are not uncommon. However, without proper positive affirmation, people will not be able to cope with this situation using an unknown reserve force that each person possesses.